I0802582

Introduction by W. Terrence Gordon

Published in *The Man-Made Object*. Ed., Gyorgy Kepes, New York: George Brazillier Inc., 1966, pages 90 – 95, this essay complements *Understanding Media* (first edition, 1964; Gingko Press edition, 2003) in a number of interesting ways:

1) It offers a new definition of the all-important concept of environment as "a special organization of available energies;"

2) It advances McLuhan's special take on the concept of translation (chapter 6 of *Understanding Media* is titled "Media as Translators") with the observation that progressively inclusive and ecological data allow us to "look at the environment as a huge teaching machine that can translate us out of the human dimension altogether. It then occurs to us that we might be able to translate, or program, the environment before it translates us;"

3) It offers explicit statements of the inherent potential of each new technology in the electronic age. — WTG

The Emperor's Old Clothes

The natural effect of any new technology is to create a new environment for itself. In effect, an environment is a special organization of available energies. As an energy system, an environment is a process. It reprocesses the earlier environments. Old environments are the nutriment of new ones. As they are assimilated by the new energy system, the older systems are transformed into art forms. From the cliché environment to the archetypal content, the new environmental system turns the old environments into anti-environments. That is one way of perceiving what a work of art is. Art as an anti-environment is an indispensable means of perception, for environments, as such, are imperceptible. Their power to impose their ground rules on our perceptual life is so complete that there is no scope for dialogue or interface. Hence the need for art or anti-environments.

Indeed, the power of the environment to be invisible and to condition, or to brainwash subjects, was what Pavlov stressed in his work, according to the recent investigations of Erwin Straus. [1] The message of Pavlov was that the stimulus cannot be a conditioner. Only a totally controlled environment effects conditioning. Such is also the message of Jacques Ellul in his book, *Propaganda*. [2] Ideology, he says, is not propaganda. Only the simultaneous use of all the available environmental technologies is propaganda. The Western world, locked in habits of fragmented and specialized perception, ignores both the meaning of Pavlov and of Ellul by insisting on translating their vision into the terms of the old technologies. From the time that Neolithic man-the-planter began to create environments one at a time by specialist extensions of his hands and arms and feet, men have always looked at a new environment as if it were the old one. We can never see the Emperor's new clothes, but we are staunch admirers of his old garb. Only small children and artists are sensuously apt to perceive the new environment. Small children and artists are anti-social beings who are as little impressed by the established mores as they are conditioned by the new.

In his *Uncommon Law*, Alan P. Herbert records a British legal case that concerned the publication of Sunday newspapers. Evidence was brought that "what is called 'news' is always an anti-social and disturbing act; that 'news' consists, as to ninety percent, of the records of human misfortunes, unhappiness and wrongdo-

---

1 Erwin Straus, *The Primary World of the Senses*, New York, Free Press of Glencoe (1962).

2 Jacques Ellul, *Propaganda*, New York, Knopf (1965).

ing, as to nine per cent of personal advertisement . . ."[3]

It has often mystified readers of the press that real news is bad news. Good news is simply not news. The ads are full of good news. Good news is a repeat of the old environment, while bad news is a probe into the new environment. Bad news reveals the lines of force in an environment, while good news tends merely to picture the situation passively. Thus the Nielsen ratings in press stories are even more whimsically destructive and sudden than those in entertainment.

It does help to look at the newspaper as a direct, exploratory probe into the environment. Seen in this light, there is more meaning in the aesthetic bonds between the poet, the sleuth, and even the criminal. For James Bond, Humphrey Bogart, Rimbaud, and Hemingway are all figures who explore the shifting frontiers of morals and society. They are engaged in detecting the social environment by probing and transgression. For to probe is to cross boundaries of many kinds; to discover the patterns of new environments requires a rigorous study and inventory of sensuous effects. The components of new environments cannot be discovered directly. Edgar Allan Poe's detective, Dupin, is an aesthete. The aesthetes were the first to use the senses consciously and systematically as probes into the environment. Walter Pater's injunction, "To burn always with a hard gemlike flame," referred to the action of the plumber's blowtorch, a technical innovation of his day.

As the visual gradient built up in the culture and technology of the seventeenth and eighteenth centuries, much accelerated by

---

3 Alan P. Herbert, *Uncommon Law*, London, Methuen (1935), p. 14.

the printing press, man lost much of the power to deal with the non-visual factors in experience.[4] The visual bias of our culture even today is such as to create a great gap between literary and scientific sectors. For the world of electric circuitry is only incidentally related to visual factors. And *The Philosophical Impact of Contemporary Physics* by Milič Čapek[5] reveals the handicaps confronting even the Einsteins in their unconscious commitments to visual culture.

The eighteenth century went so far in developing the visual gradient of its culture that realism became acceptable. The putting of the ordinary outer environment inside books and theatres for inspection and enjoyment was to go even further in the nineteenth century. But in the middle of the nineteenth century the birth of modern art occurred in several arts at once. Whereas the Romantics had developed outer landscape in poetry and painting as a means of defining and controlling inner mental states, the symbolists, by fragmenting the realistic Romantic landscapes, were able to use the pieces as heuristic probes. The probes were used to explore and define the inner landscapes that had eluded merely visual organization and detection. A similar reversal from outer to inner modalities occurred in the rise of the stream-of-consciousness technique in poetry and fiction alike. Paradoxically, stream of consciousness offered the reader a means of making rather than of matching. By pushing cinematic and photographic imagery flow to an extreme, the poets discovered the means of making a world in which all the senses participated at once. Such had been the earlier vision of the "Romantic Image," as Frank Kermode has shown in his book of that title.[6] It is a vision that is fully realized in "Among School Children" by W. B. Yeats. As the

---

4 See E. J. Dijksterhuis, *The Mechanization of the World Picture*, Oxford, Oxford University Press (1961), pp. 418 ff.

5 Milič Čapek, *The Philosophical Impact of Contemporary Physics*, Princeton, N. J., Van Nostrand (1961).

6 Frank Kermode, *Romantic Image*, New York, Chilmark Press (1963).

visual gradient of the Renaissance reached its ultimate development, the poets, from Blake and Coleridge to Hopkins and Yeats, strove to restore the unity of the imaginative life by creating a multisensuous interplay. Yeats wrote:

> I have spent my life in clearing out of poetry every phrase written for the eye, and bringing all back to syntax that is for the ear alone. . . . "Write for the ear," I thought, so that you may be instantly understood as when actor or folk singer stands before an audience.[7]

If poets and artists began to revolt a century ago against the merely visual and pictorial organization of space and experience, it is notable that the camera has revolted likewise. Cinema is not merely visual, being the joining of eye and foot. *In Our World from the Air*, E. A. Gutkind[8] has revealed the entirely structural and non-objective qualities that are released from the terrestrial surface when camera joins the airplane. At 35,000 feet the earth belongs to Picasso, and abstract *making*. At 12,000 feet, it is still in the hands of representational art, or the modes of matching. At night the urban landscape belongs to Seurat and Rouault. It is a world of light *through* rather than of light on. It is the world of TV and reverse perspective in which the viewer is the vanishing point.

Such extensions of our faculties have immediate effects on our habits of perception. This is called "negative feedback," or learned responses to new situations. The photograph revolutionized the human image as much as it changed the patterns and spaces of our cities. Indeed, the photograph gave us a push in the direction of the programmed environment. As our data become more inclusive and ecological, we naturally begin to look at the envi-

---

7 Quoted by M. C. Bradbrook in his book *English Dramatic Form*, London, Chatto and Windus (1965), p. 125.

8 E. A. Gutkind, *Our World from the Air*, London, Chatto and Windus (1952).

ronment as a huge teaching machine that can translate us out of the human dimension altogether. It then occurs to us that we might be able to translate, or program, the environment before it translates us. Oceanographers, confronting the extravagant life of the sea, are yet mindful of the equilibrium among its creatures and components. It is the maintenance of this equilibrium that initiates trains of actions and effects of "mindless ferocity." Such had been the first theories of political economy when human factors were subordinated to the Newtonian image of Nature. As we approach the stage of programming the environment itself, it becomes natural to interrupt and suspend the "mindless ferocity" of Nature by anticipating causes with consequences. It is a revolution well under way, and it is parallel to a similar revolution in education. A great shift from instruction to discovery is beginning in education. It is the shift from matching to making, from blueprint to heuristic probe. It is based on the same kind of knowledge that earlier had enabled the engineer to predict the behaviour of skyscrapers, bombs, and rockets. We can begin to program the planet itself by understanding the actions under and above its mantle.

So little did the ancients know of the make-up of their terrestrial environment that they misnamed the planet. Had they been able to perceive the extent of the waters on the earth (70.8 per cent of its surface) they might well have called it Oceanus. But their perceptions of their earthly environment were no more inadequate or deluded than the perceptions of men in other ages and cultures. It might be well to consider briefly the role of the artist in correcting the bias of environmental perception.

If we note the artistic response of the Romantics to the first mechanical and industrial age, it will help to explain the artistic response to the first electronic age. For with electric circuitry we may have come to the end of the Neolithic time of the Planter and the Wheel. The electronic age is again the age of the hunter, the nonspecialist, who can probe the entire environment. New data-retrieval systems make this total probing more and more natural.

James Joyce published *Finnegans Wake* in 1939, revealing the return of the tribal cycle for electronic man and opening the entire world of language as a Phoenix Playhouse of dramatic metamorphoses. The artistic response to the age of circuitry has been to portray new dimensions of human interdependence and new patterns of human identity. The unconscious that had long been the environment of consciousness has become the content of modern artistic awareness. The Romantics, on the other hand, had responded to the first mechanical environment of railways and factories by a nostalgic dream of the preceding agrarian technology. Has it always occurred this way? Does the content of each new environment have to be the old environment? Does the new organization of energy that is a new environment automatically process the old environment into an archetypal ideal of art? The television environment has steadily upgraded the old movie forms into sentimentally valued art forms. The medieval world got the same treatment from the Gutenberg technology. If technological changes create new environments, or new processes of energy organization, what is to be the process of the new satellite environments on our perception and experience?

It is a common observation that in the space age we do much of our lab work outside the planet. That is just a way of looking at the new environment in terms of the old one. For radio, telescopes, and space capsules are not new content for the old situation. In the same way, the computer is not a new mechanical gadget for pepping up the old mechanical environment. The computer is not mechanical at all. Electric circuitry is an organic thing, an extension of our nervous system. Our natural impulse is to ignore the environmental aspects and to try to fit it into the old situation in the style of "horseless carriage" and "wireless." But our natural response is quite helpless and irrelevant, as the history of technology testifies.

The capsule and the satellite have created a new environment for our planet. The planet is now the content of the new spaces created by the new technology. Instead of being an environment in time, the earth itself has become a probe in space. That is, the planet has become an anti-environment, an art form, an extension of consciousness, yielding new perception of the new man-made environment. Whereas the mechanical environment turned the old agrarian world into an art form, the electric technology enables us to mime or simulate the old planetary environment in our capsules. As Buckminster Fuller has pointed out, "the rocket capsule that will keep man living successfully in space for protracted periods . . . will be the first 'scientific dwelling' in history." [9] Science, quite as much as art, is concerned with the construction of anti-environments. In the electric age the anti-environments of science incorporate the nervous system. They become "responsive environments," or probes. With electric circuitry we cannot only program the entire environment

9 R. Buckminster Fuller, in *World Resources Inventory*, Carbondale, Southern Illinois University Press, Phase I Document 3, p. 90.

responsively as a work of art, we can include the learning process in the environment itself.

In his *Poetics* (Chapter IV, 1448b), Aristotle reminded us that mimesis is the process by which all men learn. He alluded to the process of making by which our perceptions simulate within us the environment that we encounter outside ourselves. It is this learning and making process that, by electric circuitry, is being extended beyond our central nervous system. The next phase of this extension will naturally concern the action of making consciousness technologically. What we have called education in recent centuries has consisted in visiting or in simulating as many earlier environments and cultures as possible. Language is unrivalled in providing the actual sensuous modalities of other environments, with their unique ground rules. Electric circuitry can become a means to bypass language and plug directly into other modes of consciousness. Already the artists have shown us the means to this end with their strategy of the "objective correlative," or an inclusive experiential control. It is a method for anticipating the effects of a contrived situation that Edgar Allan Poe previewed in his essay, "The Philosophy of Composition." Instead of being concerned with the content of the work, Poe's method points to our own time when it is possible to include the environment in the content.

With electric circuitry, all the mechanical enterprises of mankind tend to acquire reverse characteristics. Just as the educational establishment tends to shift its stress from instruction to discovery with the audience directly involved in the learning processes, so all mechanical industry tends to abandon packaging in favor of the tailor-made or custom-built service for the individual. This pattern begins to emerge in computer design procedures in architecture. It appears quite spectacularly in the world of the book and of publishing with the advent of xerography. The book was the first mass-produced object. It was the first repeatable and uniform product. The process by which this kind of product was achieved was a process soon extended to many other forms of making. The process consists in the extreme fragmentation of the ancient craft of the scribe. Printing from moveable type is not only an analytic procedure of fragmentation, but it fathered similar fragmentation in many areas of human perception and human action.

It is precisely on this process of analytic fragmentation that all the fabrics of modern production, marketing, and pricing were built. It is a process that dissolves with the advent of electric circuitry. The dissolution of this process can be illustrated from the effects of xerography on book publication. Xerography makes the reader both author and publisher in tendency. The highly centralized activity of publishing naturally breaks down into extreme decentralism when anybody can, by means of xerography, assemble printed, or written, or photographic materials which can be supplied with sound tracks.

There are many electric information services at present that permit individuals to phone for printed data on any subject whatever. Computers are ready to go to work on their specific problem, or interest. Bibliographies and printed materials from many parts of the world can be made available to the individual in a few hours. The whole tendency of xerography is to transform the book into a tailor-made, custom-built service. The way in which the book is ceasing to be a mass-produced object or commodity provides a very good index to the changing aspect of the world itself as it becomes a responsive information environment. As the specific individual need to become paramount in the new book-making, the public is drawn into the book-making process. Artists have, during the past century, been vividly aware of the ever increasing measure in which the audience shares in the creative process. This is an aspect of the "mass audience" that is frequently deplored and misunderstood by the representatives of the old mechanical culture and environment. Such people tend to see the mass audience as the mere obliteration of old landmarks, and of individual differences. They pay no attention to the increasingly creative awareness of people who are deeply involved in one another by means of electric circuitry. They are engaged in the ancient routine of regarding the patterns of the previous environment with nostalgic reverence.

The individualism of the mechanical culture and environment was paid for at the cost of much alienation from man, and work, and society. It was also accompanied by an almost total denial of participation in the creative process on the part of the public. The mechanical culture and environment produced the spectator and the consumer instead of the participant and the co-creator. Mechanized specialism permitted high virtuosity in the shaping of the art object, but such objects were denied any real role in the social life. They were classified as "art" and made peripheral to society and to individual consciousness alike. "We have no art," say the Balinese; "We do everything as well as possible." In the same way, art as a classified activity dissolves with the advent of electric circuitry. The art object is replaced by participation in the art process. This is the essential meaning of electric circuitry and responsive environments. The artist leaves the Ivory Tower for the Control Tower, and abandons the shaping of art objects in order to program the environment itself as a work of art.

It is human consciousness itself that is the great artifact of man. The making and shaping of consciousness from moment to moment is the supreme artistic task of all individuals. To qualify and to perfect this process on a world environmental scale is the inherent potential of each new technology.

Marshall McLuhan

The Emperor's Old Clothes
Marshall McLuhan - Unbound (20)

ISBN: 1-58423-051-7
Library of Congress Control Number 2005927213

Marshall McLuhan Unbound Project Editors
Eric McLuhan, W. Terrence Gordon

Published in United States in October 2005 by
Gingko Press, Inc.
5768 Paradise Drive, Suite J • Corte Madera, CA 94925
(415) 924-9615 • Fax (415) 924-9608
email: books@gingkopress.com
http://www.gingkopress.com

Design, packaging and production: Die Gestalten Verlag, Berlin
Layout and Typography: onlab, Berlin
Fonts: *Dolly* by Underware, *Bullet* by House Industries
Production: Martin Bretschneider, Vinzenz Geppert
Art direction: Robert Klanten

Made in Germany